WE

poems by

Michael Gurshtein

Finishing Line Press
Georgetown, Kentucky

WE

ACKNOWLEDGMENTS

Thank you to all the voices, old and new, that shine a light upon the path.

Publisher: Leah Huete de Maines
Editor: Christen Kincaid
Cover Art: Michael Gurshtein
Author Photo: Jessica Suhowatsky
Cover Design: Elizabeth Maines McCleavy

Order online: www.finishinglinepress.com
also available on amazon.com

Author inquiries and mail orders:
Finishing Line Press
PO Box 1626
Georgetown, Kentucky 40324
USA

Table of Contents

There, I'll meet your soul with mine.

Hephaestus

We wait on wings of dreams for our lives to begin,
Deaf to the thunderous beating of time ticking away.
The seconds pound down like hammers on the forge,
Shaping our lives into the fleeting past.
Have you not heard the roar?
While in the furious crowd or sitting on a silent riverbank,
Time opens up its folds and you can see the sparks
And feel the heat of ending coming on.
And once the smith has finished with the work,
The piece that is your life falls coldly on the slag heap,
And he begins anew his grizzly task.
All destinies end here,
But in that glimpse of Time's eternal forge
We get to shape the product that comes out.
So listen for that sound, look for the hammer's fall
And turn the mettle of your life into a winsome shape,
Lest what comes off the anvil be another lump
Of shapeless, artless form.

A Parent's Love

Did yours nurture or belittle,
Feed or starve?
Embrace your quirks and gleefully
Run down the banks of your imagination
To push you ever on toward your dreams?
Or did they fill you to the brim
With all the fears and hurts and anger
Of their own sad and shattered lives?
Do you know every intimate detail
Of their world, or did they leave
Before you spoke or walked?
Do you know them?
Love or hate them?
Exalt or fear them?
Did they do right by you?
Do you forgive them?

Ruined Foundations

We build on what is there.
The foundations that our fathers built,
The solid of the past,
We pile on top of it as if
Afraid to tear a piece away,
To lose forever that connection
And find ourselves adrift
In time and space.
How long does memory last?
A day, a week, a month
Before we break the homes they built
In order to restore as clumsily
Upon the ruins.
And years from now,
When memory has failed,
We dig the ruins up
And wonder at the sites that we have lost.

The Freaks of Progress

Here we are.
But how did we get here?
Where did we come from?
What footpath did that first curious caveman
Wander down to wind up here,
His rocks replaced with guns and fire made obsolete
By the consuming furious hellfire of the bomb?
Let us consider him some more.
His needs are simple, basic.
Food, water, warmth, protection:
Survival, in a word.
But what's this extra feeling, this incessant nudge
That drives him to explore, to risk his peril,
To stray from easy safety with the pack?
He follows a quiet voice, a voice that only he can hear
As it beckons him into the misty depths of the unknown.
His tribesmen call him freak because they do not hear the voice,
Nor feel the urge to find what lies in the undiscovered country.
Curiosity is mutation, progress is aberration,
And those who drive it freaks.
The losers and the outcasts and geniuses and madmen
Who cannot be content with status quo.
They seek the other on the outside
And push all others forever forward, forever outward
To see the sights and hear the sounds,
To prove they are not mad, that wonders are real.
To better their fellows, in a word.

We fear the truth about ourselves,
Our cracks and imperfections;
Who wants to be the first
To stand and say "I'm flawed"?
No, far more safe to close our eyes
And to ignore the truth.
But, if we dare to open them a bit
And stare into that dread eternal light,
How much is suddenly revealed!
Our cracks and flaws shine out in beauty,
Our scars and blemishes glow.
And if we stare long enough,
So long that our retinas and souls
Begin to burn in marvel at the sight,
What deeper beauty might we finally perceive?

We bleed in minutes, hours, days,
And fritter all our lives away in searches of escape.
This show, that person, no more than a circus,
But how much more we reach for that convenient noise
Than seek out the unbearable silence
Of messy, scary solitude.
We dare not see ourselves, confront Us face to face
And stare down the musty hallways of the past
At choices, indecisions, and mistakes.
That treasure trove, that frightening adventure,
Calls only to the boldest of the bold
For there is no old, musty, half-torn map
To lead us safely down that twisted maze.
And, even had we such a map in hand,
The X we stumble clumsily upon
May well be an untriggered trap,
Awaiting patiently our unwitting return.
So we stay safe, we drift through our days
With outward bound adventures,
Eschewing our own private unplumbed depths,
Returning to the same familiar caves
In which our forebears dwelled
And bred and died and never looked
Too deep into the gaping maw of inner spheres.
This lesson we pass on:
Look deep within and maybe you will find
The answers you so crave.
More likely you'll be lost.
Better to stay away.

I speak for all of us, the ordinary folks,
The ones without power and ambition.
We seek merely to live (ideally in peace)
And not be saddled with the burdens
And the strife of all the world's problems.
We, who want nothing more than quiet, ease,
A lack of pain and fear, and plenitude of joy.
We are the deafening majority of humans,
Walking around this earth confused and wondering
"Why are we here?"
Each block along our path,
Each bramble, thorn, turned-over log,
Each petty tyrant great and small,
Each mean-spirited fool and vicious scumbag
Who seeks to take from us that he may thrive
From our starvation,
All of these barriers are nothing more than
Lessons to be learned.
Will you extend a helping hand,
Or offer up a lesson to your fellow?

The Night Realm

We dream that which we know not of,
The Mind against the Will, embracing,
Stretching into the vast unknown
And basking in the wonders and the terrors
That lie beyond the pale of conscious thought.
The shadow realms we see are full
Of that eternal host of infinite ideas
That frighten us, like children
Wandering in an abandoned house,
If we but stare too closely at their splendor.
Ideas whose time has come
To shatter our vain, illusory comfort.
Ideas whose time will never come,
But neighbors to the gears of the world
Whose time is never and always -
Timeless and endless,
Mocking our petty concepts of Time.
Ideas dark and terrible,
And light and sweet,
Fancies and nightmares
Intermingled and thrown all a-jumble
Upon the screens of our internal world
Stripped bare of pretense and protection.
We fear and tremble and delight,
And willingly return each night
To walk these hallways once again
With bated breath, to watch our brains
Construct mad castles in the air,
To hear tall tales we cannot share
Except as remnants, torn and bleak,
That sound hollow as we speak.
Thus dreams make heroes of us all
Each night as we descend to sleep,
And as we wait for night to fall
We thrill at all that beckons
In the darkest deep.

Oz Abandoned

"We are the hollow men,"
The poet once accused.
But who has made us hollow?
Who yanked our guts out
With the surgical precision of a butcher
And stuffed us full of straw and lies instead?
We have become the heartless tin-men,
The brainless scarecrows, the roaring cowards,
And the man behind the curtain is not our savior.
He holds the butcher's knife, blood freshly dripping,
With piles of guts and brains and souls
Neatly arrayed, aligned by name, sex, age, and SSN.
Salvation lies not there; it lies within ourselves.
The curtained butcher is a master of illusion; still
He cannot take, by cunning or by force,
What we refuse to give.
Be kind, though your chest feels empty.
Dare to think, though your head yet bursts with straw.
Even if scared, stand tall.
Reclaim your heart, your brain,
Reclaim your soul and shine
As you were meant to be.
Reclaim your Self.
And, on the day the curtained room stand empty
And the false wizard is revealed
To be no more than just a puny, little man,
We shall know peace.
The spell will fade and our nightmares will morph
Into our dreams.

We love in blind, crazy, foolish ways
As our cracked hearts grope clumsily along
The crooked alleys of our troubled souls,
Forever praying for a lusty spark
To finally ignite our inner fire.
And what if down some dead-end alleyway,
Stuffed stories high with old, odd memories
And rubbish heaps of passions and regrets,
What if among that refuse of our lives
We dig into the past and find ourselves?
If underneath the layers and the stains
We find a mirror of our innocence
And deeply gaze into our sinful eyes,
Discovering forgotten selves within?
If we but dare to hold a steady gaze,
To let our souls bleed out all the hurt
And, purging it with gentle, soothing care
Release us from the burdens we once sought,
What's left is naked, pure, honest love
Committed to a temporary shell.
And once the fear of that shell's quick demise
Has drowned in our love's abyssal pool,
We can go forth and share our timeless gift
Until one day we all rejoin the void.

The Immigrant's Lament

We swam in the currents of time,
Borne along by the turbulent moment,
And our only goal, our only quest, was not to drown.
None taught us to traverse that treacherous current;
We felt abandoned, treading water
And fearfully eyeing the maelstrom
That threatened to swallow us whole.
A voice called out to us across the ocean.
It was a beautiful voice:
Mothering and melodious, comforting and harmonious.
She called out, saying "Swim to me, come to my shores.
Here be no monsters. No dragons will hunt to devour you.
You will not starve, you will not thirst, you will not want.
My land is plentiful and all are welcome here."
A drowning man will cling to any rope,
And time's currents in their turbulent swirling
Had already nearly drowned us to death.
So we swam for our lives.
We swam across the water and through the sky.
Many drowned. Some made it.
We washed up on her shores
Like soaked, bedraggled rats abandoning
The sinking ship of Old.
What did we find here? Oh, here be Dragons!
Robed in white and armed with ropes of their own.
Here be the monsters of our homes
Reborn with different names but hiding the same aims.
Here be starvation, thirst, and deprivation we knew so well of Old.
Yet hers was not a siren's song drawing us
From one doom to the next.
For here be one more thing,
The thing we lacked when, drowning,
We clutched so desperately to her rope.

Here be the ultimate savior: Hope.
We fled despair, the soul-wrenching, gut-crushing CERTAINTY
That nobody would come to our aid,
That seeing us dead in the street like dogs
Would rouse a cheer in those who dared to call themselves
Our neighbors.
Such was our ancient home,
Which felt as welcome as a pauper's grave.
In this new home we are not wanted still.
But here, all came as strangers,
All swam across the gulf in some day past.
The dream of this new place is just to live,
To love, to strive, to struggle and survive.
And so we dare to hope.

I Lied

I lied. Sometimes I lie.
Because the challenge of the truth
Confuses, frightens, dares to be a man
And face whatever end the truth might bring.
So, yes, I lied. I am not lying now.
I turn myself with anxiousness around
And come back to the light where I can see
Exactly what my character contains.
I lied. I now confess.
Your anger, hurt, confusion pour forth.
My only honest choice is to accept.
The truth has set me free; I will not lie again.
Until another time...

Anya, In Memoriam

I held her close when she was barely big enough to fit
Into the warm, inviting palm of my outstretched hand.
A furry ball of brown fluff with two big, soulful, beautiful brown eyes.
Those eyes would often find me through the years
And show me all the love a creature has to give.
She grew with me and Us and when the Us became no more,
Became a Me and Her, she stayed with Her.
And Her, she would not share.
I saw those brown eyes no more,
Felt their love no longer nor
Could bury my face in the brown fur,
Grown coarser now but still
Warm and inviting and smelling
Just as only home can smell.
And now she's gone.
Her warm, wet nose, her fur,
Her wagging tail and smile
And those deep, golden brown eyes
That held the deepest love
When she gazed at me.
She's gone. I wasn't there.
I got no word from Her.

Jewels

I read the splotchy pages of my past
In search of lessons that I can't describe.
They come to me in dreams, in blurry lines,
In tea leaves and in hazy summer days,
Intruding on my mind to get their due.
The gems I keep. The rest will churn and churn
Around my restless brain until one day
They turn to amber drops that I can store
In half-forgotten drawers inside my desk.
I take the amber out now and then
And revel in the sunbeams passing through,
Reflecting, scattering across the walls
The rambling story of my distant past.
The gems I hold forever in my palm
Lest I forget the lessons so hard-fought.
They are my foundation and my soul
And they will outshine me when I go.

Flow

Dirt remembers, water forgets.
The wounds of war and cataclysm
Remain for years upon the battlefield
But water, once calamity has passed,
Is placid as it ever was before.
Our bodies, born of dirt,
Can no more melt our scars
Than can the passive ground.
But let our souls be water, still and calm,
Forgiving all the grievances of old.
The ocean is serene when all is peace.

Extraordinary moments fade
Like snowflakes in a summer breeze
Returning dullness to our lives,
Condemning to banality.
But who declares it must be so?
Let every moment have its place
In the astonishing parade
Of life's eternal pageantry.
The births, the deaths, the tragedies,
The joys and laughter, the regrets,
The boring hours of our lives
Create us, shape us, nurture us.

Memento Mori

We die a little with each passing day,
We spend ourselves with every breath we take,
Expend our minds and hearts.
How many titans died at twenty five,
At thirty three, at forty eight?
And how much more could they have done by eighty?
Each morning is our last because
We never know when death will call
And our bill come due.
Begin each day with mindful intention
And end it with a reckoning.
And on the day you die (could be today)
You'll know that you have done all that you could.

As I retread the footsteps of my days
And ask myself if this is all there is,
I find great comfort in the lasting words
Of minds, great and small, from times long past.
The thoughts of Marcus, Seneca, and God
Pour endlessly through my relentless brain,
Reminders that the tortured human curse
Afflicted them as much as it does me.
Gautama suffered long to reach his goal,
And Jesus chose to die for all man's sins,
But men (no martyrs we, we lesser men)
Trudge on in timeless loops of our device.
Let us find peace in our fruitless search,
For one day, stumbling blind upon a grove,
We shall encounter all the fruit we seek
And taste, and rest, and sleep, and leave.

A Song of Gratitude

I sing my thanks for all the trivial things
Which, bustling about, we oft forget,
So when sleep fogs my brain, my soul takes wing
And travels lightly, lacking all regret.
I'm grateful to the man who held the door,
The woman who had given me the time,
My niece at play crying "more, uncle, more!",
The lover in my bed, her life in prime.
I'm grateful for the miracles I see:
The snowflakes swirling in the cold, gray air,
The joy of laughter, careless and free,
And helpful hands, extended out of care.
Give thanks, today and always, to your kin;
They are the simplest, kindest of gifts.
Let go your pride, most cardinal of sins,
And aid in sealing humankind's rifts.
We all share the long journey of this life,
Let yours pass in gratitude, not strife.

Fare Well

Close this book,
Go out and play.
All we have is this today.
To show love, to cry and pray,
Find our cause and join the fray,
Laugh, enjoy ourselves, be gay,
Walk our path and seek our way.
When the day has fallen still
And we've taken our fill
From the flowing cup of life,
Set aside the passing strife
And reflect on what you've done,
Battles lost and lessons won,
Kindness shared and friendships gained,
Lost regrets and pains unpained.
Pass into the quiet night,
Let your unbound soul take flight
And rejoin the great divine:
There, I'll meet your soul with mine.

Michael Aleksandrovich Gurshtein was born in Moscow, Russia and lived there through the fall of the Soviet Union. In 1995, his family traded the metropolitan bustle of Moscow for the peaceful quiet of small-town Colorado. Michael returned to big-city life following his time at the University of Colorado, settling in Denver, where he continues to live to this day.

Michael's life has always been strongly driven by books and theatre. Through these media, he has endlessly explored history, philosophy, science, and art, and continues to find fascination in the ongoing human conversation about what it means to be here and what makes life interesting and worthwhile. His sincerest hope is to add value with his voice to that conversation.

Michael spends his time acting, practicing martial arts, learning new languages, diving down historic rabbit holes, concocting and chasing adventures, and delving into the multi-faceted, complex nature of human relationships. By day, he sometimes masquerades as an engineer.

www.ingramcontent.com/pod-product-compliance
Lightning Source LLC
LaVergne TN
LVHW041330080426
835513LV00008B/661